KNOW YOUR SCIENCE TOOLS

LET'S USE MAGNETS

DENNIS LIU

PowerKiDS press

Published in 2027 by The Rosen Publishing Group, Inc.
2544 Clinton Street, Buffalo, NY 14224

First Edition

Editor: Noah Riccardi
Book Design: Claire Vanden Branden

Photo Credits: Cover, p. 1 Vincenzo De Bernardo/Shutterstock.com; p. 5 Garna Zarina/Shutterstock.com; p. 7 showcake/Shutterstock.com; pp. 9 (top), 9 (bottom) Craig Walton/Shutterstock.com; p. 11 vectorfusionart/Shutterstock.com; p. 13 Michael LaMonica/Shutterstock.com; p. 15 Sorapop Udomsri/Shutterstock.com; p. 17 KPixMining/Shutterstock.com; p. 19 DenPhotos/Shutterstock.com; p. 21 Wachirawit Kamai/Shutterstock.com.

Cataloging-in-Publication Data
Names: Liu, Dennis.
Title: Let's use magnets / Dennis Liu.
Description: Buffalo, New York : PowerKids Press, 2027. | Series: Know your science tools | Includes glossary and index.
Identifiers: ISBN 9781499459661 (pbk.) | ISBN 9781499459678 (library bound) | ISBN 9781499459685 (ebook)
Subjects: LCSH: Magnets--Juvenile literature.
Classification: LCC QC757.5 L58 2027 | DDC 538.4--dc23

Manufactured in China

CPSIA Compliance Information: Batch #QS27PK. For Further Information contact Rosen Publishing, at 1-800-237-9932.

CONTENTS

Magnets Aren't Magic

Magnets can push and pull things without even touching them. They can also stick to some objects. You probably have toys that are magnets. Magnets are also used in important tools. Magnets aren't magic. So how do they work?

What Makes a Magnet?

Magnets are made from special **metals**. Even rocks that have a little bit of special metal in them can be magnetic. These metals have a magnetic field. A magnetic field is the area around the magnet where the force can work.

S
N
S
N

Every magnet has two poles. These are its opposite ends. We call these the north and south poles of the magnet. North poles **attract** the south poles of other magnets, but they **repel** other north poles. South poles attract north poles, but they repel other south poles.

Opposite poles attract

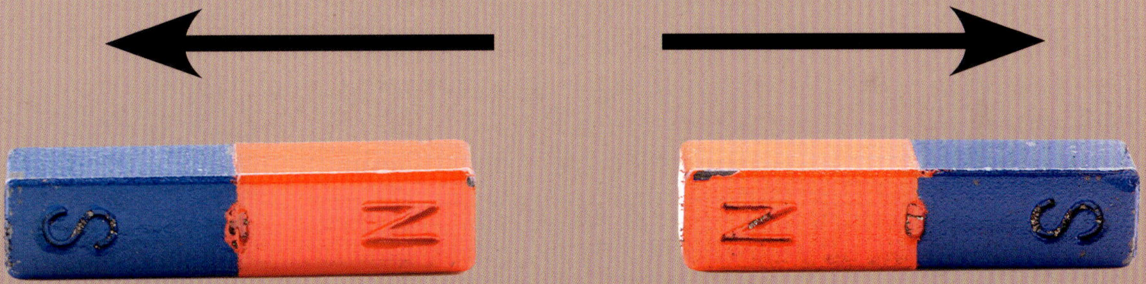

Like poles repel

Why do magnets do this? It has to do with the **atoms** that make up matter. Certain parts of atoms called electrons make a magnetic force. These electrons work together inside of magnetic metals. This gives the metals their magnetic force.

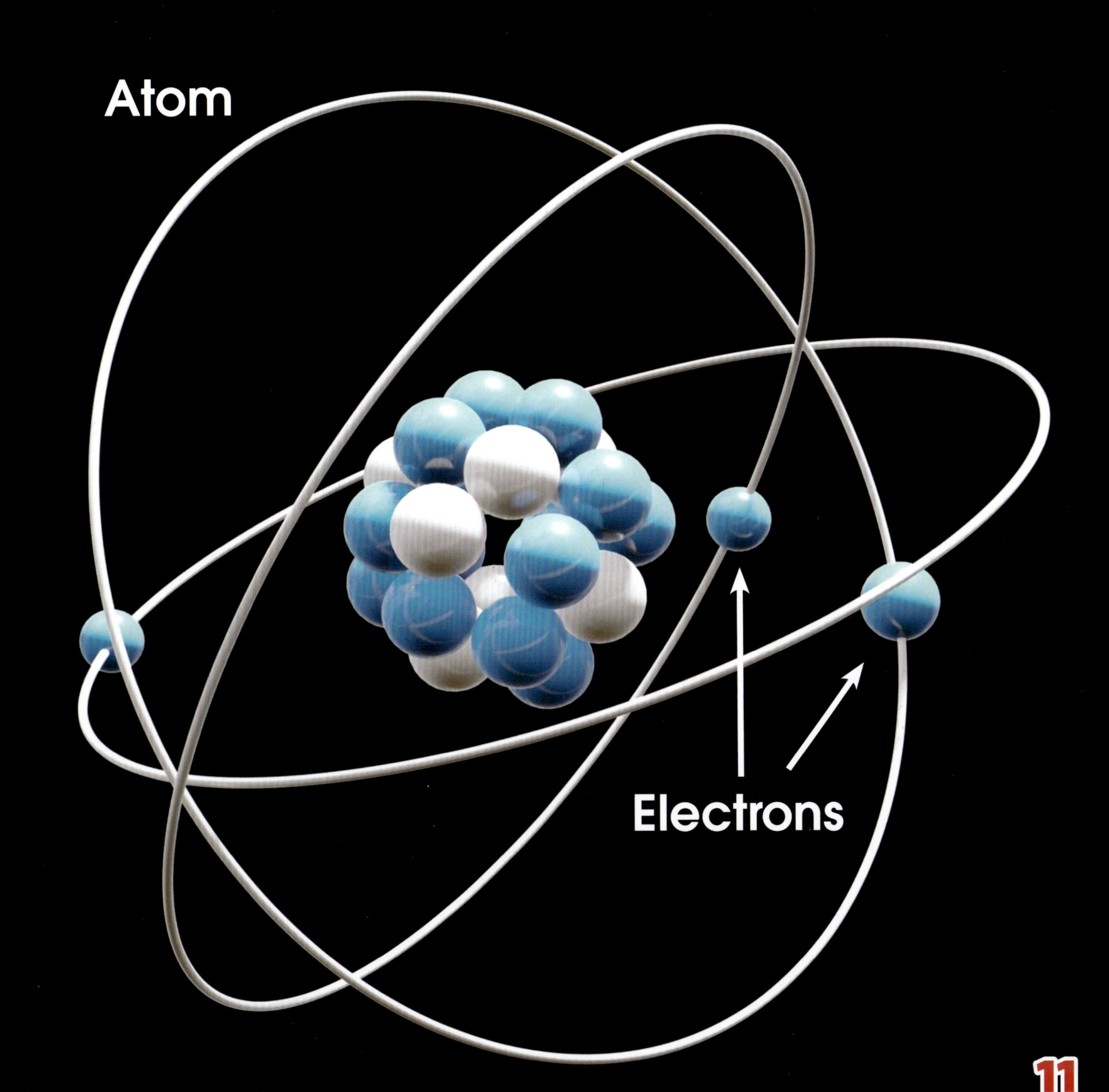
Atom
Electrons

Magnetic Materials

Some rocks are **permanently** magnetic. These are called lodestones. Some matter can become a **temporary** magnet when it touches another magnet. Iron, nickel, and cobalt are metals used to make temporary magnets. Some matter, such as wood, can never be magnetic.

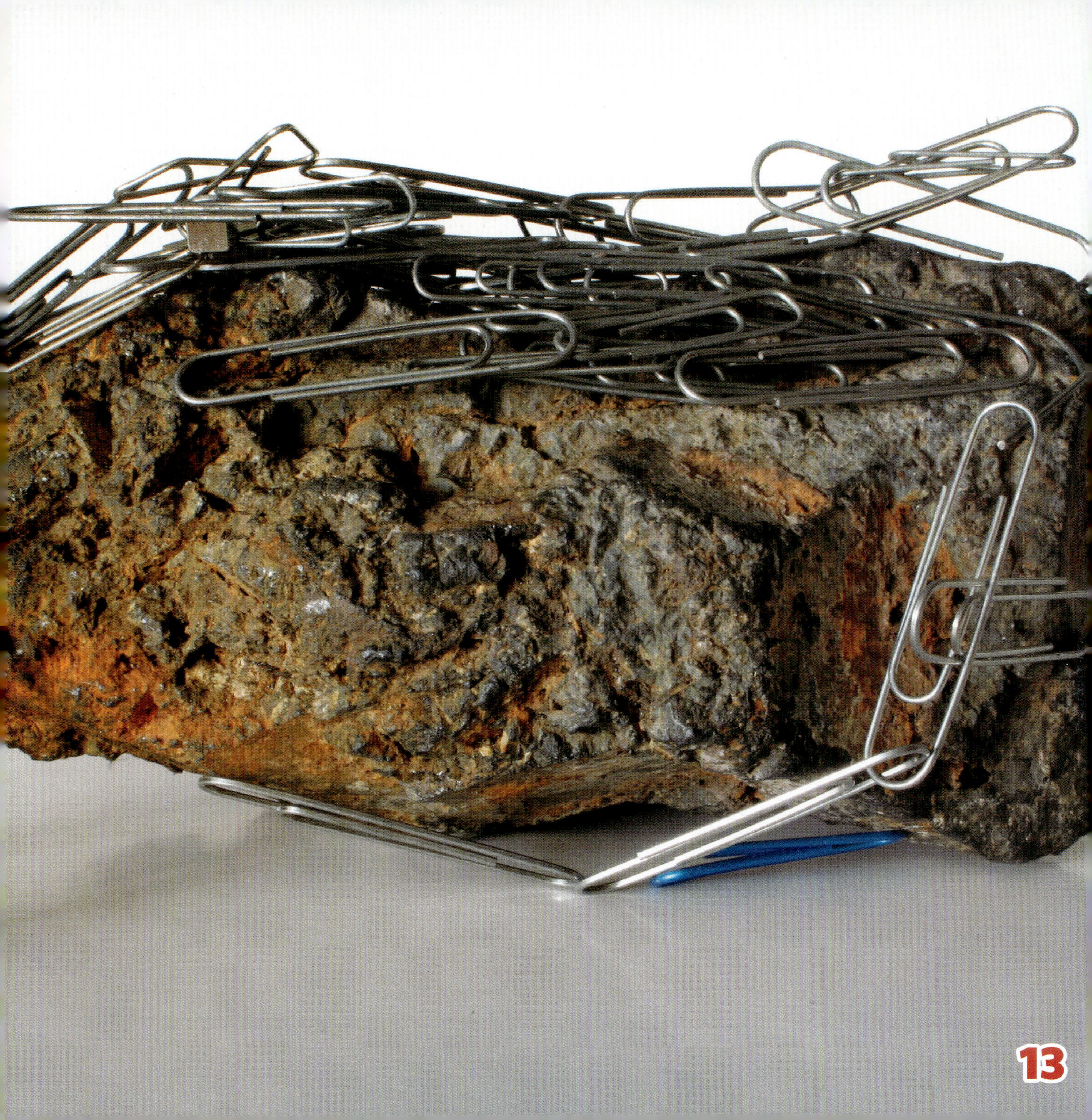

Getting Around with Magnets

Magnets can help people travel. A compass contains a magnetic needle. It points north. That's because Earth is also a giant magnet! The poles of the compass needle are attracted to the opposite poles of Earth's magnetic field.

N
NE
E
SE
S
SW
W
NW
0
20
40
60
80
220
240
260
280
300
320
340

Electromagnets Everywhere

Scientists can also make temporary magnets. They do this with **electricity**. When an electric **current** flows through a wire, it creates a magnetic field. When the wire is wrapped around a metal such as iron, it creates an electromagnet. Electromagnets are used in **motors**.

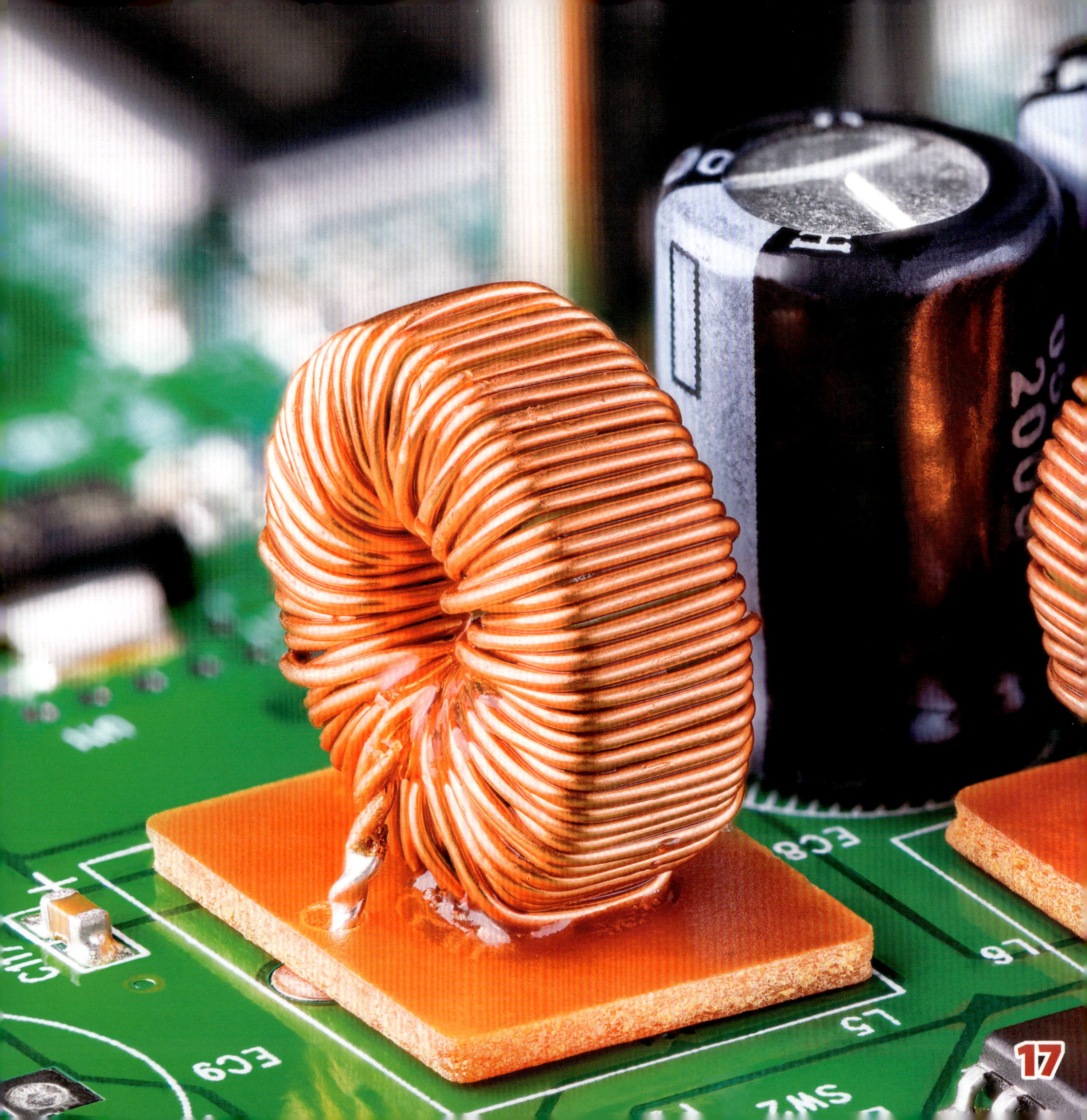
EC8
EC9
L5
L6

Electromagnets are everywhere. So many objects and tools we use every day need them to work. We often don't even realize how many. Without electromagnets, we wouldn't have toasters, telephones, or cars!

11:33
Wednesday
26
Messages
Calendar
Photos
Camera
Weather
Maps
Clock
Home
Stocks
Notes
Reminders
News
Videos
iTunes Store
Books
Files
Health
Wallet
Contacts
FaceTime
App Store
Activity
Watch
Settings

Magnets Are Amazing!

We are lucky to be able to use magnets. They allow scientists to make many of the **inventions** we use today. Maybe someday you'll be a scientist who works with magnets, too. What would you make with magnets?

GLOSSARY

atoms: The smallest bits of matter.

attract: To draw nearer.

current: A flow of electricity.

electricity: Energy that is carried through wires and is used to operate machines.

inventions: Tools created after study.

metals: Shiny elements found in the ground.

motors: Machines that produce motion or power for doing work.

permanently: Never changing.

repel: To push away.

temporary: Lasting for a limited time.

FOR MORE INFORMATION

BOOKS

Chapman, Amy. *Forces and Magnets*. Buffalo, NY: Rosen Publishing, 2025.

Harts, Marie. *Magnetism*. Buffalo, NY: Rosen Publishing, 2025.

WEBSITES

Explain That Stuff: Magnetism
explainthatstuff.com/magnetism.html
Read all about magnets and magnetism.

PBS LearningMedia: Magnets: An Invisible Force
thinktv.pbslearningmedia.org/resource/magnets-invisible-force-media-gallery/science-trek/
Learn more about how electricity and magnetism work together.

INDEX